# Freaky Flying Animals

### Earth's GROSSEST Animals

## Alix Wood

WINDMILL BOOKS

New York

Published in 2014 by Windmill Books, An Imprint of Rosen Publishing
29 East 21st Street, New York, NY 10010

Editor: Sara Howell
Designer: Alix Wood
Consultant: Sally Morgan


Photo Credits: Cover, 1, 4, 5, 6, 7, 8 bottom, 9 right, 10, 11, 14, 15, 16, 17, 18, 19, 20, 21, 23, 25 top,
26, 27, 28, 29 © Shutterstock; 3 and 8 top © Stephen Bonk/Fotolia; 9 left © Hal Brindley/Fotolia;
12  Ecoscene; 13 top © NOAA; 13 bottom © Nick Bonzet; 22 top © Sanchezn; 22 bottom ©
Alexander/Fotolia; 24 and 25 bottom © Chein Lee/Minden Pictures/FLPA

Library of Congress Cataloging-in-Publication Data
Wood, Alix.
 Freaky flying animals / by Alix Wood.
    pages cm. — (Earth's grossest animals)
Includes bibliographical references and index.
 ISBN 978-1-61533-736-1 — ISBN 978-1-61533-789-7 (pbk.) —
 ISBN 978-1-61533-790-3
1.  Animals—Miscellanea—Juvenile literature. 2.  Animal flight—Juvenile literature. 3.  Wings
(Anatomy)—Juvenile literature.  I. Title.
 QL49.W6943 2014
 591.47'9—dc23
                                    2012050220

Manufactured in the United States of America

CPSIA Compliance Information: Batch # BS13WM: For Further Information contact Windmill Books, New York, New York at 1-866-478-0556

# Contents

# Gross Animals in the Sky

They can be **ugly**, they can be angry, they can **swarm**, and they love to vomit. There are all kinds of freaky flying animals!

This ugly bird is a turkey! Its throat is covered with colored growths which turn bright red when the turkey is upset or wants to show off. It has flaps of skin that hang over its beak and under its chin. They turn red, too. Wild turkeys can fly, but many farm turkeys are just too heavy.

A swarm of up to a billion monarch butterflies arrive in the mountains of Mexico each year! They are poisonous to predators.

Flying creatures aren't all harmless. Some of the larger birds like this goose can be dangerous, especially when they are guarding their young.

This owl is coughing up a **pellet**. Owls can't chew as they have no teeth. They swallow small prey whole and tear larger prey into smaller pieces. Some hours later they cough up a pellet of leftovers!

An owl's pellet contains all the pieces the owl couldn't **digest**, like bones, fur, feathers, bills, claws, and teeth!

# Vultures Aren't Fussy

**Vultures are nature's garbage collectors. Most birds that eat meat feed on live animals, but the vulture eats the rotting bodies of the dead.**

A vulture is very useful at picking up the pieces other animals wouldn't eat, especially in hot countries where dead animals rot quickly. Vulture stomach acid is very powerful, so a vulture can safely eat rotting animals infected with diseases that would kill other **scavengers**.

If a dead animal's hide is too thick for a vulture's beak to open, it waits for a larger scavenger to eat first.

Vultures have few feathers on their head and neck to keep them clean when feeding.

Vultures won't usually eat a dead animal on the day that it is killed. They mostly feed on the second or third day when the animal has begun to rot. They rarely eat a kill on the fourth day. Scientists believe that the meat is too fresh on the first day and doesn't smell enough for the vultures to find it. On the second and third day it smells and is easy to find. On the fourth day the meat is just too rotten!

A group of 50 vultures can turn the **carcass** of a sheep or impala to skin and bones in 20 minutes!

After a meal, vultures perch in the heat of the Sun to bake off any mess on their feathers.

# Strange Bats

Bats are the only **mammal** that can really fly. Other "flying" mammals **glide**. Some bats can take off from the ground, but bats with long, narrow wings have to crawl up something first!

Bats are at home flying in the air, but sometimes they have to move around on the ground. A bat looks very strange when it crawls. It pulls itself along by its strong front legs using its claws. A bloodsucking vampire bat can run by balancing on its weak back legs and pulling itself along with its front legs. Most bats' back legs are not strong enough to do this.

claws

This horseshoe bat (right) gets its name because its nose is shaped like a horseshoe. The folds of skin on the nose focus sound when the bat uses **echolocation**. The bat makes high-pitched sounds that bounce off objects and return to the bat as echoes. Bats in flight can tell the difference in sound between a tree, your head, and a tasty grasshopper!

Bats are not blind, but most have better night vision than day vision. They see in black, white, and shades of gray.

Bat droppings are dangerous to humans. When touched they break apart into a powder. If the powder is breathed in it can cause a disease called histoplasmosis.

# Freaky-Looking Birds

These storks and vultures wouldn't win any beauty contests. Their food choices are pretty grim, too.

The large, powerful marabou stork eats pretty much anything, from rotting flesh, scraps, and animal waste. It has been known to eat just about anything it can swallow, including shoes and pieces of metal!

A marabou stork will sometimes wash its horrible, rotting food in water to remove any soil!

A marabou stork has cloak-like wings, skinny, white back legs, and a large white mass of "hair." It looks like an old man in a dark suit!

These ugly New World vultures come from North America and South America. The turkey vulture has a highly developed sense of smell. It can sniff out dead animals hidden by trees and undergrowth only an hour after the animal has died. Other species of vulture follow the turkey vulture to find food.

Vultures can't sweat. To cool off in the heat, they **urinate** on their legs!

turkey vulture

Andean condors are massive vultures. They weigh around 33 pounds (15 kg) and have a 10 foot (3 m) wingspan!

Andean condor

If a turkey vulture is threatened after it has just eaten, it vomits everything in its stomach up for the predator as a peace offering!

King vultures have powerful, hooked beaks that can tear open tough carcasses. They can often eat through hide that other vultures can't.

king vulture

# Flying Frogs and Fish

These animals seem to fly, but they actually glide. Some species of frogs and fish use this handy skill to escape predators.

Some flying frogs make foam nests by mixing **mucus** and water using their back legs. They lay their eggs in the nest over water. When the eggs hatch, the tadpoles drop into the water!

Some types of tree frog "parachute" out of the trees by using their large **webbed** feet and skin flaps on their arms and legs. The skin flaps catch the air as they fall. They can glide up to 50 feet (15 m).

Extra-large toe pads help the flying frog land softly and stick to tree trunks.

A flying fish can leap out of the ocean and use its winglike fins to glide above the water. The longest recorded glide is 1,300 feet (400 m), at a speed of 43 miles per hour (70 km/h)! The flying fish beats its tail 70 times a second and rides the upward currents of warm air that the waves make.

Flying fish have been known to strand themselves on ships by flying onto the deck!

a mobula leaping out of the water

The mobula (left) is a large ray which can jump out of the water as high as a tall man! It weighs over 1 ton (900 kg). You wouldn't want to be standing on the deck of a boat if this huge creature crashed on board!

13

# Pretty Gross Polly

Parrots are very intelligent birds. That doesn't mean they don't have some horrible habits, though, like eating with their feet and vandalizing cars!

A baby parrot isn't the prettiest creature on the planet!

In the parrot world, vomiting all over your date means true love! When a bird throws up small amounts of food it is its way of showing affection. It's very common for pet parrots to throw up on other birds, their favorite toys, or even their favorite people!

Some African gray parrots like this one are able to copy human words. They can understand what some words mean and form simple sentences. Be careful what you say around a parrot!

Parrots are the only birds that use their feet to help them eat! They use their beaks to climb, too!

Called "the clown of the mountains," the kea will often damage cars. This one is biting a car antenna.

Keas are big, clever parrots that live in the cold mountains of New Zealand's South Island. They are the world's only alpine parrot. The kea is curious, and it likes to search through people's bags, steal things, and damage cars. A kea will eat almost anything and is believed to attack sheep!

# Flying Insects

Plenty of insects can fly. The insects on these pages have some amazing tricks up their sleeves, though. One can survive being frozen alive! Another bursts out of its own skin. Yuck!

A weta is a giant, flying grasshopper found in New Zealand. The heaviest one recorded weighed as much as three mice! A weta can bite with powerful jaws and it can give painful scratches by lifting its hind legs and striking downward, aiming the spines at the eyes of any predator.

spines

A mountain stone weta can survive being frozen for months! Its body fluids contain a substance that stop ice from forming in its cells.

Adult dragonflies will eat just about any bugs they can catch. They have fierce, crushing jaws. Even their young, called nymphs, are ferocious underwater eaters. They eat tadpoles, fish, and even each other! They catch their food with a toothed lower lip.

a dragonfly eating a fly

an adult cicada coming out of its exoskeleton

Young cicadas **molt** several times as they grow underground. When they are mature they come above ground and molt for the last time to become an adult cicada. Often millions of cicadas hatch at the same time. Large swarms can harm young trees by eating their leaves and laying eggs in their branches.

# Flightless Birds

These freaky animals can't be bothered to fly. They lost their ability to fly because they either didn't need to escape predators, or they could run or swim better.

Ostriches are the biggest birds in the world. They are taller than a person and weigh about the same as a piano! It's mostly because of their size that ostriches can't fly.

Ostriches still have wings, which they use to help steady themselves when they run. They can run as fast as a greyhound!

An ostrich can be very dangerous when protecting its young.

The cassowary (right) is one of the most dangerous birds in the world. When kept in zoos it will often attack its caretakers. The daggerlike sharp claws can deliver a bone-breaking kick.

The red color of the wattle becomes paler or darker according to the mood of the bird! Cassowaries can jump up to 5 feet (1.5 m) high and they are expert swimmers.

wattle

A well-placed kick from any of these three birds could kill a human!

Male emus can be dangerous. The male incubates the eggs, and during this time he doesn't eat, drink, or go to the bathroom. He only moves to turn the eggs about 10 times a day. No wonder he's moody!

# Angry Birds and Ugly Ducks

It's not a good idea to get any of these birds angry. They will all guard their young and their territory fiercely. Even this ugly duck is big enough to cause some damage!

The Muscovy duck (right) has a body like a duck, hisses like a goose, has claws on its webbed feet, and roosts like a chicken! This large duck also has ugly red bumps on its face and a claw on each wing!

Muscovy ducks eat anything they can find! They like bugs, roots, stems, leaves, **algae**, seeds, small fish, lizards, snakes, and even mice, voles, and baby rats.

Male Muscovy ducks don't quack at all. The females make a soft giggling sound!

Geese are sometimes used to guard property. They can be very fierce and will chase, nip, and hiss at anyone who passes by. Their bites can leave bruises.

An angry goose will lower its head with beak open, hiss, and then pump its head up and down.

A mother swan will guard her young from predators. She will attack any animal that she thinks is a threat.

Swans can look so peaceful as they glide along the water, but don't get one angry. Swans attack by smashing at their enemy with the bony spurs in their wings. They also bite with their large bill. A swan's wings are strong enough to break a person's leg.

# Sea Birds

Sea birds are well-known for one revolting habit. They often drop their waste on peoples' heads! They have some other nasty habits, too.

The photo on the left shows an adult masked booby and its cute little baby. That baby isn't as innocent as it looks, though! Masked boobies lay two eggs. If both hatch, the stronger chick usually kills the weaker one. This helps the parents, though, because they have to work hard to keep one chick fed. They would have to work twice as hard to feed two chicks.

A masked booby nest is shallow, so the stronger chick can push its weaker brother or sister out pretty easily.

Baby birds can easily become some other bird's lunch. This fulmar chick (right) has a trick. It vomits an oily, orange gunk all over the face of any predator! The gunk smells like rotten fish and damages the attacker's feathers so they lose their waterproof coating and might drown.

A fulmar chick's spitting distance is an impressive 6 feet (2 m).

A puffin has been recorded holding 62 fish in its beak!

Herring gulls sometimes steal fish right out of a puffin's mouth!

A puffin uses its round tongue to push fish up into notches in its upper bill that help hold the food securely. That way, the puffin can keep its mouth open to catch more fish, adding to the collection already in the back part of its mouth!

# Gliding Snakes and Lizards

Some snakes and lizards have body parts that can catch the air and help them glide to the ground. Many rain forest animals can glide from tree to tree.

"Draco" means "dragon" and the draco lizard is great at gliding! Its ribs form a semicircle on either side of its body when it needs to glide. It folds its ribs back next to its body when not in use. Males use their gliding ability to chase rivals from the two or three trees they claim as their own.

Draco lizards have been known to glide as far as 195 feet (59.5 m). They use their long, slender tails to steer.

Snakes are scary enough, without having to worry about them flying around! A flying snake (left) can flatten its body and flare out its ribs into a "c" shape to trap air as it falls. By wriggling back and forth as it falls, it can actually steer!

**This paradise flying snake is poisonous, too!**

Flying geckos or parachute geckos can glide up to 200 feet (60 m)! The flaps on either side of its body, its webbed feet, and its flattened tail allow it to glide over short distances. It does a swoop at the end of its flight to land softly.

# Butterflies and Moths

Butterflies are so delicate and pretty. It is hard to believe they have any gross habits. Surprisingly, they have quite a few!

Butterflies need minerals and salts in their diet. To get them they will sip urine, dung, and standing water. If there's no water around, a butterfly may vomit or urinate and drink that! The butterfly will drink the same urine several times to get all the nutrients out of it.

a butterfly drinking its own urine

These butterflies are drinking from a puddle which has absorbed minerals from the soil underneath it.

Butterflies eat by sipping through their straw-like mouthparts. They like rotten fish, animal urine, human and animal waste, and rotten fruit.

a group of blue mazarine butterflies sipping manure

The luna moth, below, has no mouthparts! It never eats or drinks in its adult form. It only lives for one week, and concentrates on finding a mate.

Is it a bird? No, it's a moth! Clearwing moths mimic other creatures, like hornets, wasps, or even hummingbirds.

# Gliding Mammals

These gliding mammals are quite cute sitting still. The sifaka and its friends have some pretty funny ways of getting around, though!

The sifaka, a type of lemur, has thick hairs on its forearms and a small skin flap under its armpit. These help the sifaka glide down from the trees. When it needs to cross open ground it skips along on its hind legs with its forearms held up high for balance!

The name "sifaka" comes from the noisy barking call they make.

A sifaka has really huge big toes!

After bats, a flying lemur is the mammal best adapted for flight. Its limbs and tail are joined by large flaps of skin. Even the spaces between the fingers and toes are webbed. It can glide as far as 230 feet (70 m) with hardly any loss of height! When resting, it hangs upside down from branches by its strong claws.

skin flap

Flying lemurs are good climbers, but they are clumsy on the ground. They climb up trees in short hops.

Sugar gliders love sugary food. They can glide by using a flap of skin that extends from their front to back feet. During the cold season, a sugar glider may go into a state of **torpor** to save energy.

# Glossary

**algae** (AL-jee)
Plantlike life-forms that mostly grow in water.

**carcass** (KAR-kus)
A dead body.

**digest** (dy-JEST)
To convert food into simpler forms that can be taken in and used by the body.

**echolocation** (eh-koh-loh-KAY-shun)
A way of locating objects by making sound waves that bounce off the objects and back to the sender.

**exoskeleton** (ek-soh-SKEH-leh-tun)
A hard structure on the outside of the body.

**glide** (GLYD)
To fall freely through the air without flying.

**mammal** (MA-mul)
An animal that feeds their young with milk, have a backbone, and have skin covered with hair.

**molt** (MOHLT)
To shed hair, feathers, outer skin, shell, or horns to be replaced by a new growth.

**mucus** (MYOO-kus)
A slippery, sticky substance.

**pellet** (PEH-lut)
A wad of undigested material regurgitated by a bird of prey.

**predators** (PREH-duh-terz)
Animals that live by killing and eating other animals.

**scavengers** (SKA-ven-jurz)
Animals that usually feed on dead or decaying matter.

**swarm** (SWORM)
A large number of insects grouped together and usually in motion.

**torpor** (TOR-per)
A state of lowered bodily activity as a response to extreme cold or drought.

**urinate** (YER-ih-nayt)
Produce liquid animal waste.

**webbed** (WEBD)
Flaps of thin skin between toes and fingers.

**WEBSITES**
For web resources related to the subject of this book, go to:
www.windmillbooks.com/weblinks
and select this book's title.

# Read More

Carney, Elizabeth. *Bats*. National Geographic Readers. Des Moines, IA: National Geographic Children's Books, 2011.

Clark, Willow. *Flying Lemurs*. Up a Tree. New York: PowerKids Press, 2012.

Owen, Ruth. *Puffins*. Polar Animals: Life in the Freezer. New York: Windmill Books, 2013.

# Index